Cor... ...
to the
Order of Mass

The new translation

By
Mgr Bruce Harbert

*All booklets are published thanks to the
generous support of the members of the
Catholic Truth Society*

CATHOLIC TRUTH SOCIETY
PUBLISHERS TO THE HOLY SEE

Contents

Introductory Rites

Go therefore and make disciples of all nations, baptising them in the name of the Father and of the Son and of the Holy Spirit, teaching them to observe all that I have commanded you; and lo, I am with you always, to the close of the age.[1]

The Ascension of Christ

These are the last words that Our Lord spoke on earth to his disciples, as reported by the Gospel of Matthew.

We come to Mass to obey one of his commands, that is, to take bread and wine in his memory, as he commanded at the Last Supper, 'Do this in remembrance of me'.[2] And when we come, he fulfils in a particular way his final promise to be with us always, as bread and wine are transformed into his Body and Blood for us to eat and drink. Because of this link of continuity between Our Lord's farewell and our own eucharistic celebration, it is appropriate that the priest's opening words are taken from the last words of Jesus. We can imagine a film in which Jesus and his disciples are on the mountain of the Ascension, and as he speaks he fades from view, to be replaced on the screen by a priest in Mass vestments saying *In the name of the Father and of the Son and of the Holy Spirit.*

In the name of the Father and of the Son and of the Holy Spirit

We say these words so often during our Catholic life that it is easy for us to forget their meaning and import. Reading them in their original context in the Bible helps us to recover our lost awareness. A large proportion of the words of the liturgy are drawn from Scripture. To grow in knowledge of the Bible is the best way of deepening our understanding of the liturgy.

These are the words with which everybody is baptised. Their use at the beginning of Mass reminds us that the eucharistic assembly is a gathering of the baptised. In earlier days, the unbaptised were not allowed to be present for the whole of the celebration. Even now, when attendance at Mass is open to all, those who come without suitable preparation must surely be puzzled by what they see and hear. The Mass only makes sense in the context of the Faith as a whole, instruction in which necessarily accompanies baptism.

All of us who have been baptised into Christ Jesus, says Saint Paul, were baptised into his death; we have been buried with him by baptism (Romans 6:3-4). So it is appropriate that, as the baptismal words are uttered, we make the sign of the death of Christ, which is the sign of the Cross. We, the baptised, are those who are committed to live *no longer for ourselves, but for him who died and rose again for us,* as the Fourth Eucharistic Prayer says.[2a] The Mass is a re-entry into the mystery of Christ's death, so that it is appropriate to begin with this reminder of the instrument of his crucifixion.

Amen

The people respond with *Amen*, the first of many occasions on which they will use this word to indicate that they identify with the celebrant in what he says. At this point, they indicate that, as a baptised people, they are ready to enter again into the presence of the Lord and to identify themselves with him in his death, taking up the Cross with him.

Communion of the Holy Spirit

Saint Paul had a long and difficult relationship with the turbulent Christian community at Corinth, and wrote two letters to them. At the end of the second of these, he took his leave of them with these words:

> The grace of the Lord Jesus Christ, and the love of God, and the communion of the Holy Spirit be with you all.[3]

Just as the Church uses the last words of Jesus to his disciples, so she uses the last words of Saint Paul to the Corinthians as she begins the Mass.

The word *communion* deserves special notice. It translates the Greek *koinonia*, which is used in several senses in the New Testament. Modern translations use several different English words to translate *koinonia*, but here I have altered the Revised Standard Version, translating it by 'communion' in every case, in order to bring out the relationship among its various senses. Acts speaks of the relationship among the members of the earliest Christian community in Jerusalem as 'the communion',[4] and Saint Paul uses the same word often in a similar sense. For instance, he narrates how Peter, James and John extended the 'right hand of communion' to him and Barnabas[5]. His second letter to the Corinthians, from which our greeting is drawn, is particularly rich in such uses, motivated perhaps by Saint Paul's concern to stress the need for solidarity within the Christian community[6]. 'Fellowship', 'partnership', 'sharing' and 'solidarity' are all possible translations for *koinonia* when used in that sense, which we may call 'horizontal'.

But *koinonia* also has a 'vertical' sense, when it expresses the relationship of Christians with Christ:

> God is faithful; by him you were called into the communion of his Son, Jesus Christ our Lord[7]

To the Philippians, Paul writes of his desire for communion in the sufferings of Christ, and speaks of 'the communion of the Spirit,[8] as he does at the end of his second letter to the Corinthians in the greeting that we are studying.

The 'horizontal' and 'vertical' senses come together when Paul writes of the Eucharist, in which Christians are united both with Christ and with one another:

> The cup of blessing that we bless, is it not a communion in the blood of Christ? The bread that we break, is it not a communion in the body of Christ? Because there is one bread, we who are many are one body, for we all partake of the one bread.[9]

A brief passage at the beginning of Saint John's First Letter brings together the two dimensions of communion, and can be a useful basis for meditation on this central New Testament concept:

> that which we have seen and heard we proclaim also to you, so that you may have communion with us; and our communion is with the Father and with his Son Jesus Christ.[10]

But such communion can be destroyed:

> If we say we have communion with him while we walk in darkness, we lie and do not live according to the truth; but if we walk in the light, as he is in the light, we have communion with one another, and the blood of Jesus his Son cleanses us from all sin.[11]

For this reason it is appropriate that, as Christians gather to celebrate the Eucharist, they pray for *the communion of the Holy Spirit.*

Grace to you and peace from God our Father and the Lord Jesus Christ

Again and again in the New Testament we find the words *Grace to you and peace from God our Father and the Lord Jesus Christ.* The order of words in this greeting may seem strange: would it not be more natural to say 'Grace and peace to you'? Perhaps, but it seems that the earliest Christians used to greet one another in this way. We find this greeting in the letters of Saint Paul on no fewer than eight occasions[12], and in a shorter form in two others[13], and each time 'to you' comes between 'grace' and peace'. That phrase is found also at the beginning of each of the letters of Saint Peter[14] and at the beginning of the Book of Revelation[15]. What this seems to indicate is that the precise form of words 'grace to you and peace' was a standard greeting among the earliest Christians. Perhaps it functioned as a secret code, enabling Christians readily to identify *bona fide* members of their own community. In the New Testament, of course, we find this greeting in Greek. When the Scriptures came to be translated into Latin, the same word-order was preserved, so that when Mass is celebrated in Latin today, *Gratia vobis et pax* is the form used. More recent translations, too, have followed this tradition, for instance the King James Authorised Version and the Catholic Douai version, as well as Martin Luther's translation into German. When a priest greets the eucharistic assembly in this way, he is using a greeting that goes back to the very earliest days of Christianity.

The Lord be with you

The priest may also greet the people at the beginning of Mass with *The Lord be with you*. The Latin form of this greeting, *Dominus vobiscum*, is found only once in the Vulgate Latin Bible. Boaz, an owner of land near Bethlehem, meets some reapers on their way to gather the harvest from his fields.

...and he said to the reapers, 'The Lord be with you!'
And they answered, 'The Lord bless you.'[16]

Behind the reapers walks a group of gleaners, poor
people who collect whatever they can from the grain that
the reapers have left behind. Among these is Ruth, from
Moab, a widow who is struggling to support herself and
her mother-in-law Naomi in a foreign land. We may picture
her as haggard, because undernourished, and poorly
clothed. She may make us think of those who search for
food among the rubbish on the streets of our cities. A priest
who says *The Lord be with you*, like Boaz, does not know
who hears him. It is a greeting made to all within earshot,
however marginalised they may be.

Boaz' greeting was not directed towards Ruth, but he
notices her and enquires about her, and is impressed by
what he hears about Ruth and her care for Naomi. He
offers Ruth his protection, and soon their relationship
develops until, at the end of the book, we find Naomi
looking after little Obed, the son of Boaz and Ruth, who
are now married. Obed was to be the father of Jesse, the
father of King David, from whom Christ's own descent is
traced[17]. So Boaz' greeting, which we repeat at Mass, is a
link in the chain that leads to the Incarnation. You never
know what will happen when you say 'The Lord be
with you'.

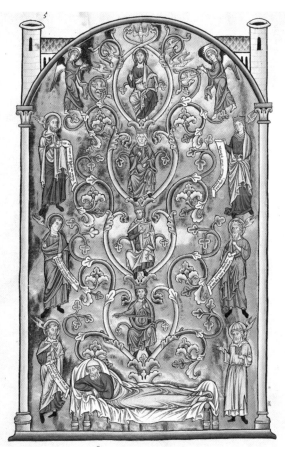

The Tree of Jesse

The Latin form of this greeting has no verb, with the result that it can correctly be translated either as a wish 'the Lord be with you' or as a statement 'the Lord is with you'.

The other greetings in the Introductory Rite are unambiguously wishes, and *Dominus vobiscum* has been translated to conform with them. But it may be noted that, whereas a priest extends his hands as he says these words, the rubrics instruct a deacon to keep his hands joined, an indication, perhaps, that he is making a statement, recognising the presence of the Lord in the assembly. Speakers of English, who use 'you' for both singular and plural, may be reminded of the Angel Gabriel's greeting to Mary, 'The Lord is with you', another link in the incarnational chain.

Who is 'the Lord' referred to here? Boaz uses a Hebrew expression that refers to God, and we must understand him to be speaking of God as understood in his time and place. But among Christians the matter is different, and there are supporters for interpreting 'the Lord' as referring to God the Father, God the Son, God the Holy Spirit, and all three Divine Persons conceived as a unity. There is no clear winner among these different views, and there probably never will be. We are free to make our own choice.

Peace be with you

As we have seen, the greetings at the beginning of Mass are taken from Scripture. But only one of them comes from the lips of Christ himself. Twice on the day of his Resurrection, John's Gospel tells us, he said to his anxious disciples 'Peace be with you'.[18] A week later, meeting them again, he said the same words.[19] Only a Bishop may use this greeting in the liturgy. This is appropriate, for the Bishop is the principal representative of Christ in his diocese. When a diocesan Bishop celebrates solemnly, with seven candles carried before him in procession, recalling the opening vision of the Book of Revelation[20], and passes between them on his way to the altar, there we have an icon of Christ, of whom that book speaks as the one 'who walks among the seven golden lampstands'. When we see the Bishop turn to us and hear from his lips the words of the Risen Lord, *Peace be with you*, then we may imagine ourselves among the Apostles on the first Easter Day.

And with your spirit

The people's response to all the greetings is the same. It is not found in Scripture. The nearest scriptural parallels are in the letters of Saint Paul, who provides the most useful key for the interpretation of these words. He takes his leave of the Galatians thus:

> The grace of our Lord Jesus Christ be with your spirit, brethren. Amen[21],

of the Philippians and of Philemon with his companions thus:

The grace of the Lord Jesus Christ be with your spirit[22],

and of Timothy thus:

The Lord be with your spirit[23].

Paul's use of 'spirit' at the end of his letter to the Galatians is particularly interesting, because he has spent a good part of his previous chapter[24] explaining what he understands by 'spirit', contrasting it with 'flesh'. This is not a contrast between the material and non-material components of human nature, but rather between what in us is directed by the influence of the Holy Spirit and what is not. Some translators of this passage print 'Spirit' with a capital letter, indicating that they understand that God's Holy Spirit is being referred to here, while others, by using a small letter, show that they consider Paul to be speaking of the human spirit. This divergence points to the fact that, for Paul, the Divine Spirit and the human spirit are very close. He writes at one point of them bearing witness together:

When we cry, 'Abba, Father!' it is the Spirit himself bearing witness with our spirit that we are children of God, ...[25]

According to P. C. Spicq, the Dominican Pauline Scholar, by 'spirit' Saint Paul means 'the spiritual part of man that is closest to God, the immediate object of divine influence, and in particular the receptacle of the Spirit of God'.

Paul lists the 'works of the flesh' as 'fornication, impurity, licentiousness, idolatry, sorcery, enmity, strife, jealousy, anger, selfishness, dissension, party spirit, envy, drunkenness, carousing, and the like'[26]. The fact that not all of these are external, bodily activities, but rather take place internally, within the mind, shows that, for Saint Paul, 'the flesh' is not synonymous with 'the body'. Nor is 'the fruit of the Spirit' purely internal, comprising as it does 'love, joy, peace, patience, kindness, goodness, faithfulness, gentleness, self-control...'[27]

When Saint Paul ends his letter to the Galatians with 'The grace of our Lord Jesus Christ be with your spirit, brethren. Amen', he is praying that Christ's grace will strengthen and foster the 'fruit of the Spirit' within them. As Paul's letter to the Galatians comes to focus on the spiritual dimension of their lives, so the people's response to the celebrant at Mass indicates that their concern is spiritual, and that what they are about to do is to be done with the inspiration of the Holy Spirit.

Saint John Chrysostom spells this out in a sermon for Pentecost:

If there were no Holy Spirit, there would be no shepherds or teachers in the Church, since they come to be through the Spirit, as Paul says: 'In which the Holy Spirit set you as shepherds and overseers'[28]. Do you see that this [i.e. the eucharistic celebration] also takes place through the Spirit? Had the Holy Spirit not been in this man, our common father and teacher, when a short while ago he went up to this holy sanctuary and gave peace to all of you, and you all answered him together, 'And to your Spirit', then, not only would you not reply with these words when he goes up, and when he speaks to you, and when he prays on your behalf, but also when he stands beside this holy table as he is about to offer that tremendous sacrifice; for... he does not touch the oblations before he himself invokes on you the grace that comes from the Lord, and you answer him, 'And to your Spirit', reminding yourselves by those words that the man who is present does nothing, and that the gifts set before you are not achievements of human nature, but that it is the Spirit's grace, present and descending on all, that prepares that mystical sacrifice. Do not therefore look to the nature of what is seen, but recognise the grace that is unseen. Of the things that take place in this holy sanctuary, nothing is human.

Some will object that Chrysostom is speaking of the gift of the Holy Spirit as if it belonged to the priest alone, but he goes on to speak of the presence of the Spirit in the Church as a whole.

If the Spirit were not present, the Church would not assemble; and if the Church does assemble, then it is clear that the Spirit is present.[29]

It is as though Chrysostom were amplifying Saint Paul's words, 'no one can say, "Jesus is Lord" except by the Holy Spirit,'[30] by adding, 'and no one can say, "And with your spirit," except by the Holy Spirit'.

Penitential Act

Saint Paul, writing to the church at Corinth, warns against receiving the Eucharist without due preparation:

> Whoever, therefore, eats the bread or drinks the cup of the Lord in an unworthy manner will be guilty of profaning the body and blood of the Lord. Let a man examine himself, and so eat of the bread and drink of the cup. For any one who eats and drinks without discerning the body eats and drinks judgment upon himself.[31]

Our Lord himself also speaks of the preparation necessary before the offering of sacrifice:

> So if you are offering your gift at the altar, and there remember that your brother has something against you, leave your gift there before the altar and go; first be reconciled to your brother, and then come and offer your gift.[32]

Let us acknowledge our sins

Appropriately, then, at the beginning of Mass the Church invites us to acknowledge our sins. *Acknowledge* means not merely to call them to mind, but to express openly our sorrow for them. We are often reluctant to do this, so the

Church helps us by putting into our mouths the words of characters we meet in the Bible. First comes King David. He is well known for his sin of contriving the death of Uriah so that he could marry Uriah's wife Bathsheba[32a] but in the formula beginning *I confess...*, we hear an echo of another moment of repentance as we say *I have greatly sinned*. These are the words of King David when, at Satan's prompting, he has conducted a census of the people and thereby provoked God's displeasure

> And David said to God, 'I have sinned greatly in that I have done this thing. But now, I pray thee, take away the iniquity of thy servant; for I have done very foolishly.'[33]

When our feelings are aroused, we tend to repeat ourselves, often making groups of three similar expressions. There are several examples of this in the Mass, beginning with *through my fault, through my fault, through my most grievous fault*. Liturgical texts, like this one, have the function, not merely of expressing how we feel but of teaching us how to feel. These words are intended to help us feel penitent.

Have mercy on us

The prayer *Have mercy on us, O Lord, for we have sinned against you* is based on a verse from the Book of Baruch[34], which is set in the time of Israel's exile from the Promised Land. It encourages the people of Israel to repent of their sins, which have caused the exile. It is useful to read through this short book, perhaps during Lent, to deepen one's sense of sorrow for sin.

All farmland needs rain, and a drought can be disastrous. Psalm 85 belongs to a time of drought: the psalmist names Israel's sin as the reason why God is withholding rain from the land. He begs God to turn from his anger, as he has done on past occasions of Israel's history. and prays that God's mercy will save them from the threat of a poor harvest. The Church borrows from this Psalm when she says *Show us, O Lord, your mercy. And grant us your salvation.*

You were sent to heal the contrite of heart

In one form of the Penitential Act, the words that the Church uses to express her sorrow for sin are derived from the words of Christ himself. Luke's Gospel tells how Jesus, at the beginning of his ministry, stood up in the synagogue of Nazareth and announced his mission in these words:

> The Spirit of the Lord is upon me, because he has
> anointed me to preach good news to the poor.
> He has sent me to proclaim release to the captives
> and recovering of sight to the blind,
> to set at liberty those who are oppressed,
> to proclaim the acceptable year of the Lord.[35]

He was quoting from the prophet Isaiah[36], but omitting the words

[The Lord] has sent me to bind up the broken-hearted

which recall those of the Psalmist:

[The Lord] heals the broken-hearted,
and binds up their wounds.[37]

These are the Old Testament passages that inspire the Church when she says to Christ *You were sent to heal the contrite of heart.*

You came to call sinners

Jesus was well known as a healer, and his healings drew great crowds to him, but he insisted that physical healing was not the ultimate goal of his ministry. Criticised by the Pharisees for eating with tax-collectors and sinners in the house of Matthew, also called Levi, who was himself a tax-collector, Jesus uses sickness as a metaphor for sin when he replies:

"Those who are well have no need of a physician, but those who are sick.[38]

He continues:

I came not to call the righteous, but sinners.[39]

thus giving us the second invocation in this form of the Penitential act: *You came to call sinners.*

You are seated at the right hand of the Father to intercede for us

Soon after his arrest in the Garden of Gethsemane, Jesus was brought before the High Priest and his collaborators, who asked him whether he was the Messiah. According to Mark he replied 'I am'[40], whereas Matthew and Luke tell us that his response was less direct. All three agree, however, that he went on to prophesy that the Son of Man would be seated at the right hand of God.[41] Saint Paul repeats this image, speaking of the working of God's great might,

> which he accomplished in Christ when he raised him from the dead and made him sit at his right hand in the heavenly places.[42]

> If then you have been raised with Christ, seek the things that are above, where Christ is, seated at the right hand of God.[43]

and speaks of Christ interceding for us at his place in heaven:

who is to condemn? Is it Christ Jesus, who died, yes, who was raised from the dead, who is at the right hand of God, who indeed intercedes for us?[44]

May almighty God have mercy on us, forgive us our sins, and bring us to everlasting life

Note the difference between *May almighty God have mercy on us, forgive us our sins, and bring us to everlasting life* and the formula of sacramental absolution, where the priest says 'I absolve you from your sins'. This formula does not suffice for the absolution of mortal sins, for which confession to a priest in the Sacrament of Penance is necessary. [45]

Lord, have mercy. Christ, have mercy

Lord, have mercy. Christ, have mercy. Lord, have mercy: These invocations are sometimes understood as all addressed to Christ, as in the form of the Penitential Act that has just been considered. At other times they are addressed to the three Divine Persons in turn. Here is an example from the Middle Ages, whose opening words, *Lux et Origo*, have given their name to a Gregorian chant setting that belongs particularly to Eastertide:

Supreme God, light and source of light, have mercy,
Kyrie eleison
On whose will all things always depend, have mercy

Kyrie eleison
Who alone can show us mercy,
Kyrie eleison.
Redeemer of humankind and their salvation, in kindness
have mercy,
Christe eleison.
Redeemed by the Cross from unending death we pray
you, have mercy,
Christe eleison.
Word of the Father, sower of love, light of truth, have
mercy,
Christe eleison.
God the Holy Spirit the Paraclete, on us have mercy,
Kyrie eleison
Our medicine and our mercy, have mercy,
Kyrie eleison
Trinity and Unity, on us always have mercy,
Kyrie eleison.

The Greek word for mercy, *eleos*, is very similar to the
word for 'olive', *elaia*, which led some of the Fathers to
draw a parallel between God's mercy and the soothing
powers of olive oil. Saint John Chrysostom offers us a
meditation on this theme, which may be found useful in the
context of the annual Chrism Mass, or indeed of any Mass,
since the celebrant always leads the people in begging
God's mercy:

There is nothing that pleases God so much as mercy. That is why priests, kings and prophets were anointed with this (oil): they considered olive oil to be a symbol of God's love for mankind. Moreover, they realised that a ruler must have more mercy. Oil showed that the Spirit is to come to man by way of mercy, since God has mercy on human beings and loves them. 'But thou art merciful to all, for thou canst do all things,[46] says the Scripture. That is why they were anointed with olive oil. He also established the priesthood out of mercy, and kings were anointed with oil. Anybody who wishes to praise a ruler can find nothing more suitable to speak about than mercy, for mercy belongs to authority.[47]

Gloria, Collect, Word

Glory to God

When Jesus was born in Bethlehem, Luke's Gospel tells us, shepherds heard angels singing in the sky:

> Glory to God in the highest heaven,
> and on earth peace among men with whom he is pleased![48]

The Church makes their song her own on most Sundays and on feast-days, singing:

> *Glory to God in the highest,*
> *and on earth peace to people of good will.*

Although modern translators interpret the original Greek of the second line as above, when the Bible was translated into Latin many centuries ago, its final phrase was understood to mean 'people of good will', an expression that has passed into common parlance. The Vatican document that guides translation of the liturgy, *Liturgiam authenticam*, requires that the Latin text be translated, not its source,[49] and that well-known expressions that have been adopted into popular language from the liturgy be retained.[50] For those reasons, this version of the angelic hymn differs from those found in modern scriptural translations.

The Adoration of the Shepherds

The *Gloria* is a hymn and so, like any other hymn or song, reveals its character best when sung. Simply to recite its words is to deny it its true character. Sung texts often contain repeated words, phrases or patterns, just as music itself involves repetition. A look through any contemporary hymnbook will provide many examples. A person who attends Mass in a foreign language will understand little or nothing of what is said, but will often be able to recognise the familiar patterns of texts like this, and gain from them a sense of the universality of the Church's liturgy, whatever the language used for its celebration. The *Gloria* also occurs in liturgies of the Greek tradition, though not in the Eucharist.

On earth peace

The rhythm of *and on earth peace* is somewhat irregular, since both 'earth' and 'peace' are stressed syllables. The translators have generally tried to avoid such collocations, preferring a regular alternation of stressed and unstressed syllables. It would be possible to write 'and peace on earth to people of good will', thus achieving a five-stressed iambic line as used by Shakespeare, Milton and many other English poets, which trips easily from the tongue. However, both the Latin and the Greek texts of the angelic hymn place 'on earth' before 'peace', thus giving added emphasis to the latter, and this pattern has been followed in the English translation.

We praise you

There follow no fewer than five verbs expressing the attitude of the worshippers to God the Father, *We praise you, we bless you, we adore you, we glorify you, we give you thanks,* a pattern that conveys a sense of exuberant enthusiasm. These are followed by three divine titles, or four, depending on how they are counted: *Lord God, heavenly King, O God, almighty Father.*

The next paragraph is addressed to God the Son, who is honoured with no fewer than five titles. Like the Father, he is addressed as God, but his titles also express his relationship with Father: *Lord Jesus Christ, Only Begotten Son, Lord God, Lamb of God, Son of the Father.*

Lamb of God

Now the hymn changes key, as it were, and a tone of pleading replaces one of exultation. We shall meet the title *Lamb of God* several times during the Mass. It originates from the words of John the Baptist as reported by John's Gospel: John was near the River Jordan, baptising his followers, when

> ...he saw Jesus coming toward him, and said, 'Behold, the Lamb of God, who takes away the sin of the world'![51]

John's words echo those of Isaiah, which the Church reads in her liturgy of Good Friday, applying them to Christ:

Surely he has borne our griefs
and carried our sorrows...
he was wounded for our transgressions,
he was bruised for our iniquities;
upon him was the chastisement that made us whole,
and with his stripes we are healed...
the Lord has laid on him
the iniquity of us all...
like a lamb that is led to the slaughter,
and like a sheep that before its shearers is dumb,
so he opened not his mouth.[52]

John also echoes Jeremiah:

But I was like a gentle lamb
led to the slaughter.
I did not know it was against me
they devised schemes, saying,
'Let us destroy the tree with its fruit,
let us cut him off from the land of the living,
that his name be remembered no more.'[53]

At the right hand of the Father

Now the tone changes again, returning to one of exultation, as
the hymn evokes the image of Christ enthroned at the Father's
right hand, which has already appeared in the Penitential Act,
and will appear again in the Niceno-Constantinopolitan
Creed: *you are seated at the right hand of the Father.*

The movement from the minor key of the central section to the major key of the opening is completed when we begin to praise Christ *alone*, and again the triple repetition of that word heightens the emotion. 'Alone' may seem surprising, since Christians worship Christ with the Father and the Holy Spirit, but this tension is resolved as they are brought in to accompany him in the last two lines. Nevertheless, the Holy Spirit may seem to be brought in almost as an afterthought. This pattern is found in many early Christian texts that focus on the Father and Son with less attention paid to the Spirit. It is known as Binitarian, in distinction from the Trinitarian pattern which gives more equal prominence to all three Divine Persons. This issue will arise again in connection with the Niceno-Constantinopolitan Creed.

Amen

The *Gloria* has taken the Christian assembly on a journey from praise to supplication and back. They affirm their identification with both these approaches to God by concluding their hymn with *Amen*.

The Collect

Latin has more than one word for 'pray'. The word that the Missal uses before the Collect – *oremus* – refers specifically to praying aloud in public. Saint Cyprian wrote:

> Our prayer is public and communal, and when we pray, we do not pray for one person, but for the whole people, for we, the whole people, are one.[54]

Cyprian was thinking specifically of the Lord's Prayer, but his words apply to most liturgical prayer.

Nearly every Collect consists of a single sentence. However, the body of the Collect ends with a full stop, and the conclusion begins with a capital letter, even though together they form one sentence. This shows that the punctuation of liturgical texts has distinctive conventions, arising from the fact that they are designed to be sung. The full stop at the end of the body of the prayer reminds the celebrant to inflect his voice at this point, and the capital letter indicates that a new musical section is beginning, usually with *Through our Lord...*

The unity of the Holy Spirit is the bond that unites God the Father and God the Son, as a hymn in the Liturgy of the Hours says:

> Father, in majesty enthroned,
> Thee we confess with thy dear Son.
> Thee, Holy Ghost, eternal bond
> of love, uniting both in one.[55]

Although Christ is the subject of the early part of the sentence that concludes the Collect, that is, the one who *lives and reigns*, when we reach *one God*, we must assume that the subject has changed, for we cannot speak of Christ as 'one God' alongside the Father and the Holy Spirit: this phrase must be taken to refer to all three Divine Persons considered as a unity.

The Word of the Lord

'Word' in English usually means a single element of vocabulary, such as 'cat' or 'hear'. Less frequently we use it to refer to an entire utterance, as when we say 'the word got about' or 'the word on the street'. We use 'word' in the same way when we speak of Christ as the Word of God, following Saint John's Gospel: he is not a single word uttered by God, but God's self-expression. This is what we listen to in the Liturgy of the Word.

The Latin Missal has the same formula at the end of all the readings: *Verbum Domini*, which means *The Word of the Lord*. The different formula at the end of the Gospel in the English version, *The Gospel of the Lord*, helps to remind the congregation that their response is different from the one made at the end of non-Gospel readings.

Note that 'The Word' does not refer to a printed text, or to the book that contains it, but to God's word as it is proclaimed aloud to the listening congregation. This acclamation may remind of us as such expressions in Scripture as 'the word of the Lord came to Abram',[56] 'Hear the word of the Lord'[57]...'The word of the Lord came to me'[58] and 'the word of the Lord abides for ever'[59] as well as of Our Lady's response to Gabriel 'let it be to me according to your word'[60] and the opening of John's Gospel: 'In the beginning was the Word'.[61]

When the Gospel is read in Church, Christ is present and speaking to us. The Second Vatican Council said:

> Christ is always present in His Church, especially in her liturgical celebrations. ... He is present in His word, since it is He Himself who speaks when the holy scriptures are read in the Church.[62]

For this reason we acclaim Christ at the end of the Gospel, *Praise to you, Lord Jesus Christ*, just as we acclaim him after the Consecration, when he is newly present on the altar sacramentally.

The Niceno-Constantinopolitan Creed

The longer of the two Creeds used at Mass derives from one that was agreed on at the Church's first Ecumenical Council, the Council of Nicaea, in the year 325. The bishops at that Council were concerned to express a correct understanding of the relationship between God the Father and God the Son, and so they gave little attention to God the Holy Spirit. Their Creed ended with '... and in the Holy Spirit'. Everything that follows those words in our Creed was added later, as will be explained below. For a fuller study of the Creed, consult Part 1, section 2 of the *Catechism of the Catholic Church*.

This Creed was not intended for liturgical use, and only gradually began to be used at Mass. Whereas the Council Fathers at Nicaea had begun their Creed with 'We believe...', the liturgical form of the Creed, in East and West, begins with the singular 'I believe'. Saint Thomas Aquinas wrote:

> The profession of the faith is handed on in the Creed as if by a single person, that is, the whole Church, united by faith.[63]

and the Catechism says:

> Whoever says 'I believe' says 'I pledge myself to what we believe.' Communion in faith needs a common language of faith, to be normative for everybody and to unite everybody in the same confession of faith.[64]

The Niceno-Constantinopolitan Creed in the original Greek, and in the official Latin translation, begins with a very long sentence. For ease of understanding and proclamation, the English translation has broken this Creed into four sections, each beginning *I believe*.

For us men

With the words *for us men* we assert that Christ became human for the salvation of all human beings. We use the word 'men' as it is often used, to refer to the entire human race. If we were to say simply 'for us', the words could be taken to indicate only a certain group within the human race, for instance all Catholics or all Christians. Christ became incarnate for everybody.

The Council of Nicaea met in order to refute the teachings of Arius, who regarded Christ as a creation of God the Father. Denying this, the Council asserted that the substance, that is, the being, of Christ is identical with that of the Father. That is the meaning of the technical term *consubstantial*.

The Lord, the giver of life

The words *the Lord, the giver of life* begin the section of the Creed that was added by the Council of Constantinople in 381, when disputes had arisen in the Church concerning the Holy Spirit. The Fathers of Constantinople, unlike those of Nicaea, took care to use language drawn from Scripture. The first two titles applied to the Holy Spirit are from Saint Paul:

Now the Lord is the Spirit[65]
... the Spirit gives life[66]

With *who proceeds* ... we may compare:

the Spirit of truth, who proceeds from the Father[67]

and with *who has spoken through the prophets*,

no prophecy ever came by the impulse of man, but men moved by the Holy Spirit spoke from God.[68]

To confess

'Confess' is most often used to denote acknowledgement of some misdeed, but it can also mean 'acknowledge' with no connotation of wrongdoing. This is the sense used when we say *I confess one baptism*. It has given us the term 'confessor' for one who professes the faith in the face of opposition.

The Apostles' Creed

The Apostles' Creed is the basis of Section Two of Part One of the *Catechism*, entitled 'The profession of the Christian Faith' (sections 198-1065). Refer to the *Catechism* for an extended commentary on this Creed.

The word *hell* has two meanings: (1) The abode of those who are damned for all eternity. This is the hell depicted by the poets Dante (in his *Inferno*) and Milton (in *Paradise Lost*). (2) The abode of those who lived justly and died before Christ, and were liberated by him in the time between his Death and Resurrection. This episode has been frequently represented in Christian Art, and was known in England as the 'Harrowing of Hell'. The second of these senses is the one intended here. The current translation of the *Catechism* renders this phrase as 'He descended to the dead'. The meaning is the same as that of the version used at Mass.

Offertory

During the latter part of the twentieth century, some people said that there should be no talk of sacrifice or offering at this point in the Mass. They argued that it is during the Eucharistic Prayer that the sacrifice of Christ is offered, and that consequently sacrificial language should wait until then. In consequence, this part of the Mass was widely known as the 'Preparation of the Gifts', although it has never had that title in the Missal, and when new prayers were composed to accompany the laying of the bread and wine on the altar, they said simply 'through your goodness we have received bread/wine'.

In fact, the earliest records of the Roman Rite do contain sacrificial language, used as the altar is prepared. When bread and wine are placed on the altar, we are offering to God his own gifts, for him to transform both them and us. This theme is expressed in some of the Prayers over the Offerings, for instance:

> Receive our oblation, O Lord,
> by which is brought about a glorious exchange,
> that, by offering what you have given,
> we may merit to receive your very self.
> Through Christ our Lord.[69]

It will become for us the bread of life

The words *It will become for us the bread of life* are based on words spoken by Our Lord after he has fed the Five Thousand, as recorded in the Gospel of John: 'I am the bread of life'[70]. They mean, therefore, that the bread will become Christ himself.

Blessed be God for ever

The response *Blessed be God for ever* is based on two passages in Saint Paul's letter to the Romans, where he speaks of the Creator 'who is blessed for ever'[71] and of Christ, 'who is God over all, blessed for ever'.[72]

Mixing wine and water

The prayer that the deacon or priest says as he mixes wine and water in the chalice echoes the Collect for Christmas Day:

O God, who wonderfully created the dignity
of human nature
and still more wonderfully restored it,
grant, we pray
that we may share in the divinity of Christ,
who humbled himself to share in our humanity.

It is highly likely that the author of this prayer was Pope Saint Leo the Great (died 461). During Leo's papacy, there was much controversy throughout the Church concerning the relationship between the divine and human natures of

Christ. It is necessary to understand that Christ is both truly and fully divine and truly and fully human: that is how he unites human beings to the life of God. An important clarification of this doctrine was made in 451 by the Council of Chalcedon, to whose debates Leo's writings made a crucial contribution. The Christmas collect quoted above, and the priest's prayer as he mixes water with wine, clearly reflect Leo's thinking and almost certainly betray his authorship.

The collect is found in the Veronese Sacramentary, the oldest substantial collection of prayers used at Mass in the city of Rome that has come down to us. Because of Leo's influence on it, it has sometimes been known as the Leonine Sacramentary, but scholars now agree that Leo was neither the author nor the compiler of the whole collection. This book, copied in the seventh century, but not printed until 1735, contributed much material to the reform of the liturgy after the Second Vatican Council. More recently, many more prayers from the Veronese Sacramentary were introduced in the Third Edition (2002) of the post-Conciliar Missal as Prayers over the People.

Spiritual drink

The phrase *spiritual drink* is inspired by the passage where Saint Paul, before beginning a section of teaching on the Eucharist, reminds the Christians of Corinth about Israel's journey through the desert:

... all ate the same spiritual food, and all drank the same spiritual drink. For they drank from the spiritual rock that followed them, and the Rock was Christ.[73]

The 'spiritual drink' to which the liturgy refers here, then, is the drink given by Christ, and indeed, it is Christ himself, who said 'my blood is drink indeed'.[74]

The three young men in the fire

For the Jewish people in Old Testament times, the place of sacrifice was the Temple in Jerusalem. Its establishment had been a great achievement, and it remained a focus of national pride. Imagine the grief, then, when the Temple was destroyed and a large part of the population of Jerusalem was deported into exile in Babylon. The writings of the Old Testament prophets show much concern with this disaster, and the Book of Daniel has given us some words that we use at Mass. We shall approach them by way of their context.

King Nebuchadnezzar set up a statue of himself in Babylon, and required all its residents to venerate it, including the Jewish exiles who were living there at the time. But three Jewish boys, Shadrach, Meshach and Abednego, refused, and as a punishment were cast into a blazing furnace. Far from being burnt alive, they began to sing. Their song is to be found in the third chapter of the Book of Daniel, and begins:

Blessed art thou, O Lord, God of our fathers, and
worthy of praise;
and thy name is glorified for ever.[75]

It is a striking beginning: the boys are in danger of
death, and yet they praise God for all that he has done. But
there are more surprises to come. They go on to say that
the Exile is justified, because Israel has sinned:

For thou art just in all that thou hast done to us,
and all thy works are true and thy ways right,
and all thy judgments are truth.[76]

Then, remembering that they are far from Jerusalem and
its Temple and all its apparatus of daily sacrifice, they pray
that on this day they themselves will be a sacrifice
acceptable to God:

Yet with a contrite heart and a humble spirit may we be
accepted,
as though it were with burnt offerings of rams and bulls,
and with tens of thousands of fat lambs;
such may our sacrifice be in thy sight this day,
and may we wholly follow thee,
for there will be no shame for those who trust in thee.[77]

These are the words that the Church has made her own.
The priest says them when he has laid the bread and wine
on the altar:

The three young men in the fire

With humble spirit and contrite heart
may we be accepted by you, O Lord,
and may our sacrifice in your sight this day
be pleasing to you, Lord God.

The use of the boys' words in the Mass implies that Christians similarly offer themselves as a sacrifice. The words *our sacrifice* refer, not only to the sacrifice of Christ that is about to be offered sacramentally, nor only to the bread and wine that have already been offered, but to what the Second Vatican Council called the 'spiritual sacrifices' of the faithful[78], that is, to the entire life that Christians try to live

no longer for themselves but for him who for their sake died and was raised.[79]

In the days when Christians were persecuted in Rome, they used to celebrate Mass underground, in the catacombs. On the wall of one of these is a painting of three outlandishly dressed young men – Shadrach, Meshach and Abednego, whose striking attire is explicitly mentioned in the Book of Daniel[80]. The existence of this painting, and its proximity to the altar, shows that Christians have linked that story with the Eucharist from very early times, a tradition that is continued every time we celebrate Mass.

Washing of hands

As the priest washes his hands, he repeats a verse from the great penitential psalm, Psalm 50, often known, from its first word in Latin, as the *Miserere*. A tradition relates that this psalm was composed by King David in penitence after he had committed adultery with Bathsheba. This is the second time that the Mass borrows David's words to express sorrow for sin, the first being *I have sinned greatly* in the *'I confess'*.

May the Lord accept the sacrifice

As has already been said, each person brings to Mass a different sacrifice, the offering of a Christian life with the renunciations that that involves. That is why the priest does not say 'our sacrifice', but *my sacrifice and yours*: his own sacrifice is different from the sacrifice of each other worshipper.

In their response, the people speak of a single sacrifice, the sacrifice of Christ, to which all their individual sacrifices are united by the Mass: *May the Lord accept the sacrifice at your hands*. This brief dialogue recalls the teaching of the Second Vatican Council:

> Through the ministry of the priests, the spiritual sacrifice of the faithful is made perfect in union with the sacrifice of Christ.[81]

Preface

The dialogue that precedes the Preface is one of the oldest parts of the Liturgy. It is recorded from the middle of the third century, is used in many different Eucharistic rites, and has come down to us in several languages, sometimes with small variations. Our Latin version, *Sursum corda*, can be translated in several ways. Literally it simply means 'up hearts'. This can be understood either as a command or an invitation, and *sursum* can mean either 'upwards' (denoting motion) or 'above' (denoting rest).

Lift up your hearts

So we have four possible literal translations:
• Move your hearts upwards.
• Let us move our hearts upwards.
• Let your hearts be above.
• Let our hearts be above.

The Greek text currently used by the Orthodox differs slightly from ours. Greek Orthodox priests in England say:

Let our hearts be on high.

In the 1960s, before ICEL's translations came fully into use, the following form of the priest's words was used:

Let us lift up our hearts.

This was appropriate for the Roman Rite, where the priest charactistically issues invitations, leaving it to the deacon to give instructions. But in the late 1960s and early 1970s, the International Consultation on English Texts was influential throughout Anglophone liturgical circles. They preferred the version that Thomas Cranmer had put into his Book of Common Prayer. Cranmer abolished the liturgical role of the deacon at Mass, leaving the priest to issue both invitations and instructions. So our priests say:

Lift up your hearts.

The people respond to his command

We lift them up to the Lord.

They could no less accurately respond:

We hold them before the Lord

or, with the Greek Orthodox,

We have them with the Lord.

These translations put the congregation one step ahead of the priest: they tell him that they are already doing what he has suggested or commanded.

In the new translation an opportunity has been lost here to set a more level playing-field between priest and people. But in the next phase of the dialogue this is not so.

The priest says:

Let us give thanks to the Lord our God.

This translation is simple and unproblematic. So is the response:

It is right and just.

These five words may seem brief and clipped, but we should not take them out of context. The priest begins the Preface:

It is truly right and just, our duty and our salvation...

picking up the cue that the people have given him. This time, the playing-field is level.

Christ and the Angels

There is a great variety of Prefaces in the Missal. This is one of the features that distinguishes it from the Missal used up to the time of the Second Vatican Council, which had very few, and it returns to an earlier tradition. Some early liturgical books contain huge numbers of Prefaces. They give thanks to God for many reasons and in many ways, always with Christ at the centre as the one through whom God manifests his goodness. Towards the end of each Preface, the priest begins to speak of the angels, but that does not mean that Christ is left behind because, as the Catechism says, 'Christ is the centre of the angelic world: they are *his* angels'.[82] As we prepare to welcome Christ sacramentally present among us, we remember the angels who surround him. Scripture and Tradition speak of many distinct orders of angels. Sometimes at the end of the Preface they are mentioned in a simple way, for example:

And so, with all the Angels, we praise you,
as in joyful celebration we acclaim:

whereas at other times they are enumerated more fully:

... through Christ our Lord.
Through him the Angels praise your majesty,
Dominions adore and Powers tremble before you.
Heaven and the Virtues of heaven and the blessed
   Seraphim
worship together with exultation.

The Sanctus

The Preface comes to its climax as we join with the angels in singing the *Sanctus*. This is drawn from the sixth chapter of the book of Isaiah, where the prophet has an overwhelming vision of the glory of God in the Jerusalem Temple:

In the year that King Uzziah died I saw the Lord sitting upon a throne, high and lifted up; and his train filled the temple. Above him stood the seraphim; each had six wings: with two he covered his face, and with two he covered his feet, and with two he flew. And one called to another and said:

'Holy, holy, holy is the Lord of hosts;
the whole earth is full of his glory.'

And the foundations of the thresholds shook at the voice of him who called, and the house was filled with smoke. And I said: 'Woe is me! For I am lost; for I am a man of unclean lips, and I dwell in the midst of a people of unclean lips; for my eyes have seen the King, the Lord of hosts!'[83]

The same song is heard again, in a slightly different version, in the Book of Revelation, where it is sung by four winged creatures resembling an ox, a lion, a human being and an eagle:

Holy, holy, holy, is the Lord God Almighty...[84]

It was probably this passage that suggested the insertion of the word 'God' into the text of Isaiah to give us our *Sanctus*.

Hosts

Hosts means 'armies'. Western Christians are accustomed to seeing angels depicted as winged messengers, but in the East there is a stronger tradition of representing them as soldiers, as they appear in the Book of Revelation:

Now war arose in heaven, Michael and his angels fighting against the dragon;[85]

In the Scriptural occurrences of the *Sanctus*, it is a statement about God, whereas the English liturgical version makes it an address to God. In fact, the Latin and many vernaculars make the first line a statement: 'Holy, holy, holy is the Lord...' and then begin to address him with 'heaven and earth are full of *your* glory'. The English-speaking world, influenced by the International Consultation on English Texts, has adopted the version of Thomas Cranmer.

Hosanna

Hosanna is a greeting based on Psalm 118:25, where it means 'save us'. It is used in the liturgy of Judaism as well as of Christianity, and seems to have lost much of its original meaning and become a simple acclamation. It was used by those who greeted Jesus at his triumphal entry into Jerusalem:

> And the crowds that went before him and that followed him shouted, "Hosanna to the Son of David! ... Hosanna in the highest!"[86]

In the highest indicates that both heaven and earth greet the Lord as he comes to his altar.

When Jesus entered Jerusalem before his Passion, the event we commemorate on Palm Sunday, the crowds cried out:

> Blessed is he who comes in the name of the Lord![87]

Their words were taken, like 'Hosanna', from Psalm 118, a song of triumph after victory. There is irony in their use of these words, for Jesus was on his way to the apparent defeat of Calvary. But they were pointing to the truth, since Jesus' death on the Cross was in fact a victory, to be crowned by the glory of the Resurrection. For that reason, this Psalm has always been closely associated by Christians with Easter. Saint Peter used a verse from it when preaching soon after the first Christian Pentecost:

> This (i.e. Jesus) is the stone which was rejected by you builders, but which has become the head of the corner.[88]

We use the same Psalm to greet the Gospel at the Easter Vigil, and another verse from it to greet the Gospel throughout Easter Week:

> This is the day which the Lord has made;
> let us rejoice and be glad in it.[89]

It is appropriate, then, that as we prepare to recall the Death and Resurrection of the Lord, and to greet him in his sacramental presence on the altar, we acclaim:

> *Blessed is he who comes in the name of the Lord.*

The Roman Canon
First Eucharistic Prayer

Quotations from this form of the Eucharistic Prayer are first found in the writings of Saint Ambrose in the fourth century. Over the next two centuries it seems to have undergone changes until, by the reign of Pope Saint Gregory I (590-694) it had reached a form close to the one we know today. For many centuries it was the only Eucharistic Prayer used in the Roman Rite. It came to be known as the Roman Canon.

Around the time of the Second Vatican Council, some scholars argued that the Roman Canon was unsatisfactory and should be abandoned because of its apparently fragmentary character, and because it lacked a clear Epiclesis or invocation of the Holy Spirit. Pope Paul VI decided that the Roman Canon should be retained in the revision of the Missal after the Council, but that it should be supplemented with other Eucharistic Prayers.

Language of prayerful humility

This Prayer is composed in a more complex style than the others, showing the Roman love of rhetorical elaboration. This is immediately apparent from the opening paragraph:

To you, therefore, most merciful Father,
we make humble prayer and petition
through Jesus Christ, your Son, our Lord:
that you accept and bless
these gifts, these offerings,
these holy and unblemished sacrifices.

The use of two or more terms for the same thing ('prayer and petition'; 'gifts ... offerings ... sacrifices') or action ('prayer and petition') removes this language far from the patterns of ordinary everyday speech. This repetitious style may remind us of the *Gloria*. It invites us to put worldly considerations aside, and to adopt an attitude of careful humility before God as we move into the central part of the Mass.

Be pleased to grant her peace: 'be pleased to', which occurs frequently in the Missal, translates Latin *digneris,* which can also be translated 'deign to', though many people consider that translation too remote from contemporary usage to be appropriate for the liturgy. Its function is to soften a request to God, ensuring that the request does not sound like a command. It is part of the language of deference that we find throughout the Mass, and especially in this Eucharistic Prayer.

Holding to the truth translates *orthodoxis*, which can also, of course, be translated 'orthodox', but that might be misconstrued as a reference to the Orthodox churches of the East. The focus here is on the world-wide Catholic church, descended from the apostles and united around the person of the Pope, the successor of Peter.

Sacrifice of praise

The Letter to the Hebrews is a response to the second destruction of the Temple at Jerusalem, which took place at the hands of the Roman army in 70 A.D. The author reminds his readers that Jesus offered his sacrifice away from the Temple, outside the city, and encourages them to follow him:

> So Jesus also suffered outside the gate in order to sanctify the people through his own blood. Therefore let us go forth to him outside the camp and bear the abuse he endured. For here we have no lasting city, but we seek the city which is to come. Through him then let us continually offer up a sacrifice of praise to God, that is, the fruit of lips that acknowledge his name.[89a]

Thus, they are encouraged to make the sacrifice of their praise a substitute for the Temple sacrifices. The Roman Canon takes over this phrase, *sacrifice of praise,* and gives it a double application, referring it first to the praise that we offer to God during the Mass, and secondly to Christ's sacrifice of himself, offered to the praise of God, to which the Mass unites us.

Paying their homage to you echoes the beginning of Psalm 65:

> Praise is due to thee, O God, in Zion;
> and to thee shall vows be performed...

The idea is that by celebrating Mass, we are only fulfilling the duty laid upon us at our baptism.

In communion

The section beginning *In communion* is closely connected with what immediately precedes and belongs to the same syntactic unit. The use of a capital letter at the beginning of the section does not indicate the start of a new sentence, but is a tradition dating back to the days of manuscript, when capital letters were used differently.

The word *communion* reminds us of its use in one of the greetings at the beginning of Mass. Hitherto the church on earth has been the focus of the prayer, but now the *communion* of saints becomes central. First, *Our Lady* is named and adorned with titles of singular honour. Then comes *Saint Joseph*, whose name did not appear in the Canon until it was inserted by Blessed Pope John XXIII in 1962. Twelve Apostles are named, with Saint Paul making up the number in the absence of the defector Judas. They are followed by group of saints of the early Church, from Rome and elsewhere. *Linus, Cletus* (also known as Anacletus) and *Clement* are listed immediately after Peter in early lists of Popes. Scholars disagree as to whether Sixtus is Sixtus I (c.116-c.125), about whom little is known, or Sixtus II (257-258), who was martyred while celebrating the liturgy during the persecution instigated by the Emperor Valerian. *Cornelius* was Pope from 251 to 253. His name is linked with that of his contemporary *Cyprian*, bishop of Carthage (near modern Tunis) because they collaborated closely and exchanged many letters.

Lawrence, a deacon of the Roman Church, was present at the martyrdom of Saint Sixtus II, and was himself martyred four days later. Little is known about *Chrysogonus*, a martyr from Aquileia in North-Eastern Italy, whose cult soon spread to Rome, where there is an ancient church dedicated to him. *John* and *Paul*, both Romans, are venerated in a church built in their honour on Rome's Coelian hill. *Cosmas* and *Damian* are thought to have been physicians and twins: their church is in the Roman Forum. Their reputation for miraculously healing the sick led to their being nicknamed '*anarguroi*', that is, 'the silverless ones' because, unlike conventional physicians, they charge no fees.

The Latin that underlies *We ask that through their merits and prayers ... we may be defended* could more literally be translated 'Grant to their merits and prayers that ... we may be protected'. That is, we ask God to grant us his protection in response to the merits and prayers of the saints.

Spiritual offering

Latin has more words than English to express the concept of sacrifice, which occurs frequently in the texts of the Mass. *Oblation*, though not common in ordinary English speech, has been used on several occasions to avoid the monotony that would arise from overuse of 'sacrifice' and its more familiar synonyms.

The ancient Roman concept of family included all those subject to the authority of a single man, whether as blood-relatives or as servants. Often 'household' is a better translation of Latin *familia* than 'family'. We are praying here more as servants than as family-members in the modern sense, so we ask God to accept the offering of *our service, that of your whole family.*

The Latin word translated here as *spiritual* is *rationabilem*, which can often be translated as 'reasonable' or 'rational'. These would be strange epithets to apply to an offering, however. The translators have borne in mind the words of Saint Paul:

> I appeal to you, therefore, brethren, by the mercies of God, to present your bodies as a living sacrifice, holy and acceptable to God, which is your spiritual worship.[90]

The Greek word here translated 'spiritual' can also be translated 'reasonable', like Latin *rationabilem*. Pope Benedict XVI has commented on this verse, pointing out what it implies for Christian worship. It makes a close connection between spiritualness and reasonableness, so that manifestations of the irrational or disordered side of human nature are foreign to the liturgy.

By making this prayer, the priest calls down the Holy Spirit on the offerings. This moment is known as the *Epiklesis*, the 'calling-down'. We shall see that in other Eucharistic Prayers the Epiklesis is more developed.

He took bread

The original texts recording the Last Supper indicate that Jesus took a single individually cooked piece of bread. In English this is often called a 'loaf'. But it would not seem appropriate to say that Jesus took a loaf, because that term is more usually applied to raised bread than to the flat kind that Jesus used. So English cannot fully and accurately represent the meaning of the original at this point: *he took bread* can sound as though Jesus took some bread broken or sliced from a larger piece, whereas it is important that the bread he took had been cooked as a single piece, which he then broke and distributed to the Twelve. Saint Paul brings out the implications of this when he says:

> Because there is one loaf, we who are many are one body; for we all partake of the one loaf.[91]

That is, the oneness of the loaf is a sign of the oneness of the Church.

The narrative of Our Lord's institution of the Eucharist is based on Scripture. In the Roman Canon it is elaborated with characteristically Roman rhetoric, such as the description of Jesus' hands as *holy and venerable*, which intensifies the sense of mystery surrounding the event.

There is no indication in the scriptural narratives of the Last Supper that Jesus gave thanks *with eyes raised to heaven*. This detail has been introduced from Luke's story of the feeding of the five thousand, where Jesus looks up to heaven before breaking the five loaves and two fish.[92]

This is my body

It is unclear from the Latin whether, when Jesus *said the blessing*, he was blessing God or the bread. This is so in Eucharistic Prayers I, III and IV. In English translation, Jesus 'says the blessing' in Prayers I and III, and blesses the bread in IV, just as he blesses the bread before distributing it in Luke's narrative of the feeding of the five thousand.[92a] He says *eat of it*, inviting each of those present to eat some of the single piece of bread that he has just broken, and he gives the reason: *for this is my Body*.

The precious chalice

Precious chalice has been much discussed. The phrase is drawn from Psalm 23:5, which is accurately translated in modern versions as 'my cup overflows'. But the old Vulgate text is more complex, accurately rendered by the

Douai Bible as 'my chalice which inebriateth me, how goodly it is'. Here, it is not the cup that is spoken of, but its contents, for a vessel can never inebriate, whereas the wine it contains can. Accordingly, some have argued that it is not the chalice that is described as 'precious' in the Roman Canon, but the fine wine that it contains, fulfilling the prophecy of Isaiah:

> On this mountain the Lord of hosts will make for all
> peoples a feast of fat things, a feast of wine on the lees,
> of fat things full of marrow, of wine on the lees well
> refined.[93]

The use of the word *this* indicates how closely the action of the priest is identified with the action of Christ.

A distinction is traditionally made between 'everlasting', which implies an endless duration of time, and 'eternal', which implies existence unbounded by time. The sixth-century Christian philosopher Boethius defined eternity as 'the complete, simultaneous and perfect possession of endless life'. Hence, the covenant instituted by Christ, which opens for us the way to eternal life, is called *the new and eternal covenant*.

It is unclear whether it is the chalice or Christ's blood that will be *poured out*. The translation allows for both possibilities.

... for you and for many should not be taken to imply that Christ did not die for all human beings. Matthew's account of Jesus' institution of the Eucharist has him say:

Drink of it, all of you, for this is my blood of the covenant, which is poured out for many for the forgiveness of sins.[94]

and Mark has:

"This is my blood of the covenant, which is poured out for many.[95]

Compare also Isaiah:

he bore the sin of many, and made intercession for the transgressors.[96]

The mystery of faith

The phrase the *mystery of faith* was for many centuries part of the form for the consecration of the chalice. After the Second Vatican Council it was decided to remove it from that position and use it to introduce an acclamation addressed by the people to Christ newly sacramentally present on the Altar. 'Faith' here does not mean the subjective virtue of faith, the faith *with* which we believe, but the faith *that* we believe, that is, the Faith's objective content. The phrase is drawn from Saint Paul's first letter to Timothy:

Great indeed, we confess, is the mystery of our religion:
He was manifested in the flesh,
vindicated in the Spirit,
seen by angels,
preached among the nations,
believed on in the world,
taken up in glory.[97]

In this translation, 'our religion' is used to bring out the objective character of what is being affirmed.

The first two Acclamations are both based on the words of Saint Paul:

For as often as you eat this bread and drink the cup, you proclaim the Lord's death until he comes.[98]

Both contain a forward-looking note: at Mass we both remember the past and look forward to the future, to the second coming of Christ. In the early centuries, a common belief among Christians was that the Lord would come again to his Church as she celebrated the Eucharist, particularly during the Paschal Vigil. The Lord was thought of as 'the dawn from on high' (Luke 1:78), and so Christians, when celebrating the Eucharist, turned to the East, to the rising of the sun, to greet him.

Save us, *Saviour of the world* is an antiphon from the Liturgy of the Hours for the Feast of the Exaltation of the Holy Cross (September 14). Its Latin text has been set to music by many composers. The opening Latin words of this Acclamation, *Salvator Mundi*, are the title of an image of Christ with his right hand raised in blessing and his left hand holding an orb, representing the world of which he is Saviour. Many great artists have painted this image.

The word *memorial* is rich in significance. It does not simply mean something that reminds us of the past, like a war memorial. Rather, a memorial in the theological and liturgical sense means an action that brings the past into the present, making it effective afresh. Thus, when we make the *memorial* of Christ's Death and Resurrection, those events become newly powerful for us here and now.

With *your holy people*, compare:

> But you are a chosen race, a royal priesthood, a holy nation, God's own people, that you may declare the wonderful deeds of him who called you out of darkness into his marvellous light.[99]

The holy Bread of eternal life is drawn from the words of Our Lord himself after his feeding of the five thousand:

> Jesus said to them, "I am the bread of life; he who comes to me shall not hunger, and he who believes in me shall never thirst. ...
> I am the bread of life.[100]

The Chalice of everlasting salvation comes from the Psalter:

What shall I render to the Lord
for all his bounty to me?
I will lift up the cup of salvation
and call on the name of the Lord.[101]

Acceptable sacrifice

The three Old Testament characters named in the next paragraph are all mentioned in the Letter to the Hebrews. Abel and Abraham are cited as examples of faith, and Melchizedek's priesthood is compared to that of Christ.

Abel, a son of Adam and Eve, was a shepherd. He had a brother, Cain, who was an arable farmer. The fourth chapter of the Book of Genesis tells how Abel's sacrifice was acceptable to God, whereas Cain's was not. As a result, Cain killed Abel.[102] The epithet *just* is drawn from the Epistle to the Hebrews, which comments thus:

By faith Abel offered to God a more acceptable sacrifice than Cain, through which he received approval as just, God bearing witness by accepting his gifts.[103]

Abraham was commanded by God to sacrifice his own son, Isaac, on Mount Moriah. Abraham made the necessary preparations, and took Isaac up the mountain, but at the last moment he was commanded by an angel not to hurt the boy, and a ram was found in a nearby thicket to take his place.[104] Because of Abraham's obedient faith, the Letter to the Hebrews speaks of him as though he had actually sacrificed the boy:

> By faith Abraham, when he was tested, offered up Isaac, and he who had received the promises was ready to offer up his only son.[105]

Consequently, the *sacrifice of Abraham* can be understood to refer either to Isaac or to the ram that God provided in Isaac's place.

Melchizedek is spoken of as a priest, even though he lived before the Jewish priesthood was instituted:

> And Melchizedek king of Salem brought out bread and wine; he was priest of God Most High. And he blessed him and said,
> 'Blessed be Abram by God Most High,
> maker of heaven and earth.'[106]

Because Melchizedek was neither descended from a family of priests, nor the father of a line of priests, his priesthood is compared in the Letter to the Hebrews to the priesthood of Christ himself. The author quotes the Psalm:

> You are a priest for ever after the order of Melchizedek.[107]

Melchizedek's offering of bread and wine has long been seen in Christian tradition as prefiguring the Eucharist.

Abraham, Isaac and Melchisedech

Many churches contain representations of one or more of these three figures who are connected with the Mass. A famous example, dating back to the sixth century of the Christian era, is the church of San Vitale in Ravenna, N.W. Italy, where mosaics of Abel, Abraham and Melchizedek decorate the walls near the altar.

Altar in heaven

God's *altar in heaven*, featured in the next paragraph, is the focus of much of the action of the Book of Revelation:

> And another angel came and stood at the altar with a golden censer; and he was given much incense to mingle with the prayers of all the saints upon the golden altar before the throne;[108]
> Then the sixth angel blew his trumpet, and I heard a voice from the four horns of the golden altar before God,[109] Then I was given a measuring rod like a staff, and I was told: 'Rise and measure the temple of God and the altar and those who worship there,[110]
> And I heard the altar cry,
> 'Yea, Lord God the Almighty,
> true and just are thy judgments!'[111]

It is at this altar that we ourselves participate when we celebrate Mass: our earthly altars are forgotten, and we gather at God's heavenly altar to take our share of what is offered there. The phrase *this participation at the altar* is based on Saint Paul:

> ... are not those who eat the sacrifices partners in the altar?[112]

Commemoration of the dead

The tone of the Commemoration of the Dead is calm and confident: this is the atmosphere of the catacombs, where so many of the tombs bear pictures of doves or olive-branches, or the inscription 'in peace'. The more highly-charged attitude to death that has been associated with the Roman Rite, particularly with the sequence *Dies Irae*, came later. The Second Vatican Council ordered that the revised Funeral Rites 'should express more clearly the paschal character of Christian death.[113]

The saints

The second list of saints begins with four men who appear in the New Testament but are not counted among the Apostles: *John the Baptist, Stephen, Matthias, Barnabas,* and then eleven martyrs, four male and seven female.

Ignatius was bishop of Antioch in the late first and early second Christian century. He was arrested and taken to Rome, where he was martyred, probably in 108 A.D. He wrote several *Letters*, which are among the glories of early Christian literature and show a highly developed theological understanding of Christ and of the Church.

Alexander, Marcellinus and *Peter* are early Roman martyrs, of whom little is known.

Felicity was a slave in the service of *Perpetua*. They were put to death together in the arena at Carthage on March 7, 203. A vivid account of their martyrdom survives.

Agatha and *Lucy* were both from Eastern Sicily, the former from Catania and the latter from Syracuse. Their dates are uncertain.

Agnes, Cecilia and *Anastasia* have all been venerated as martyrs in Rome from the early fourth century, though it is by no means certain that they were born or died in that city.

Conclusion

Through whom you continue to make all these good things echoes the assertion in the Niceno-Constantinopolitan Creed that *through him* (i.e. Christ) *all things were made*.

The phrase *in the unity of the Holy Spirit* has already been encountered in the Conclusion to the Collect, where it was pointed out that this is the unity that binds together the divine Father and Son. Here, while retaining that meaning, the same phrase has an additional meaning, for *the unity of the Holy Spirit* is also the bond that unites the Church. So in the Doxology that concludes all the Eucharistic Prayers the Church recalls the dual action of God's Holy Spirit, within the Godhead and in the Church. Compare:

> ... to him be glory in the church and in Christ Jesus to all generations, for ever and ever. Amen.[114]

Second Eucharistic Prayer

This Eucharistic Prayer is derived in part from one that survives from the mid-Third Century in a document known as the *Apostolic Constitutions*. Fragments of it have come down to us in many languages, and its textual tradition is very complicated. Though the name of its author was long believed to be Hippolytus, this now seems unlikely. The old text has been radically revised in order to conform to modern ideas of what a Eucharistic Prayer should be. In particular, before the Consecration an Epiclesis was added, in which the priest calls down the Holy Spirit on the bread and wine.

The descent of the Holy Spirit is compared to the *dewfall*, that is, to the silent action of dew as it settles on grass. The Post-Communion prayer in the Votive Mass of the Holy Spirit uses the same theme:

> May the outpouring of the Holy Spirit
> cleanse our hearts, O Lord,
> and make them fruitful by the inner sprinkling of his
> dew. Through Christ our Lord.

Saint Ambrose speaks of the water of baptism as the 'dew of the Spirit' whose moisture enables the baptised to extinguish the fiery arrows of the enemy.[115] Saint Peter Chrysologus writes:

> May the Spirit come like the dew. The Lord comes bringing with him moisture from heaven, and so we who were thirsty now drink and inwardly partake of that divine Spirit.[116]

Hildegard of Bingen writes concerning the Incarnation:

> The Holy Spirit touched the flesh of the Virgin with his gentle warmth, ... just as dew gently falls on grass, so that a flower, that is, the Son of God, might take human form in the flesh of the same Virgin.[116a]

Note that Jesus *entered willingly into his Passion*: he did not merely accept it, but it was the object of his deliberate choice.

The Acclamation is followed by a brief form of the Anamnesis or 'remembering', in which the Paschal Mystery is recalled. This is a standard feature of Eucharistic Prayers.

Prayer for the Church

Next comes the second Epiclesis, in which the priest prays that the Holy Spirit will come down on the assembly to unite them. The focus of the prayer then widens to include the whole of the universal Church. With the *fulness of charity* compare:

> If we love one another, God abides in us and his love is perfected in us.[116b]

The word translated in the Missal as *minister*, which is found already in the *Apostolic Constitutions*, implies priestly service. As they minister to God by participating in the Mass, the people exercise their baptismal priesthood.

All the clergy is not an entirely satisfactory translation. In English 'clergy' tends to be used as plural, so that we say 'the clergy pray' rather than 'the clergy prays'. In the Latin original a singular noun is used, indicating that all the clergy are conceived of as a single body. 'The whole body of the clergy might convey the sense of the original more fully.

The words *united with your Son in a death like his*, are closely modelled on words of Saint Paul:

> For if we have been united with him in a death like his [i.e. Christ's], we shall certainly be united with him in a resurrection like his.[117]

The 'death' referred to here is baptism, as is clear from Paul's immediately preceding words:

Do you not know that all of us who have been baptised into Christ Jesus were baptised into his death? We were buried therefore with him by baptism into death, so that as Christ was raised from the dead by the glory of the Father, we too might walk in newness of life.[118]

The hope of the resurrection is the hope given to us by the resurrection of Christ, which is our hope that we shall rise again with him.

All who have died in your mercy is a somewhat puzzling phrase, which may mean 'all whom you have mercifully caused to die' or 'all who have died trusting in your mercy'.

The light of your face is a phrase that occurs several times in the Psalms. 'Face' is often translated 'countenance':

Lift up the light of thy countenance upon us, O Lord![119]
Blessed are the people who know the festal shout, who walk, O Lord, in the light of thy countenance,[120]
Thou hast set our iniquities before thee,
our secret sins in the light of thy countenance.[121]

It is Saint Paul who tells us that we are *co-heirs to eternal life*:

When we cry, 'Abba, Father!', it is the Spirit himself bearing witness with our spirit that we are children of God, and if children, then heirs, heirs of God and fellow heirs with Christ...[122]

Third Eucharistic Prayer

The Third Eucharistic Prayer is largely the work of a single Italian monk, Dom Cipriano Vagaggini, a fine liturgical scholar who was active in the middle and later twentieth century. Around the time of the Second Vatican Council, when some were urging that the Roman Canon be removed from the Missal, Vagaggini published his suggestions for a new Eucharistic Prayer that would incorporate elements from the Roman Canon. Eventually, Pope Paul VI decided that the Roman Canon would be retained, but augmented with other Eucharistic Prayers. Vagaggini's proposals thus became the basis of what we now know as the Third Eucharistic Prayer. Because of Vagaggini's deep familiarity with the Scriptures and the Liturgy, there is nothing idiosyncratic about this prayer. Rather, it is securely based in Tradition.

God gathers his people

It begins with a paragraph that sets out the central theme of the prayer as a whole: God's unceasing work of gathering a people to himself. In this paragraph, both God the Father and God the Son are referred to as *Lord*. This may seem confusing, but it is important. In addressing Jesus as 'Lord', his disciples were giving him the name that was usually reserved to God, the 'name which is above every other name'[123]. To call both Father and Son 'Lord' is to indicate that both of them are God. In the Niceno-Constantinopolitan Creed we apply the title 'Lord' to the Holy Spirit with the same implication.

It may also seem strange to say *all you have created rightly gives you praise*, since not all things are alive in the biological sense. But the notion that the inanimate creation joins in the praise of God is found in the Psalms:

The heavens are telling the glory of God;
and the firmament proclaims his handiwork.[124]

and in the Canticle that the Church uses at Morning Prayer on Sundays:

Bless the Lord, all works of the Lord, sing praise to him and highly exalt him for ever. Bless the Lord, you heavens, sing praise to him and highly exalt him for ever.[125]

Hence, we are able to say later in the same paragraph, *you give life to all things and make them holy.*

A pure sacrifice

The prophet Malachi wrote in response to a situation of corruption and disorder in the Jerusalem Temple. In his book, God expresses disgust at the Temple worship, comparing it unfavourably to the worship offered him by other nations:

I have no pleasure in you, says the Lord of hosts, and I will not accept an offering from your hand. For from the rising of the sun to its setting my name is great among the nations, and in every place incense is offered to my name, and a pure offering; for my name is great among the nations, says the Lord of hosts.[126]

Christians soon began to see this passage as a prediction of the Eucharist, offered throughout the world. So we say:

you never cease to gather a people to yourself,
so that from the rising of the sun to its setting
a pure sacrifice may be offered to your name.

The opening paragraph has sketched the context within which the Eucharist is celebrated. *Therefore* indicates that this global situation motivates us to celebrate it here and now, asking God the Father to send the Spirit who sanctifies all things to make holy the gifts that lie on the altar. But there is another motive to be mentioned: the *command* of Jesus Christ himself, in response to which the mysteries are celebrated, wherever and whenever they are celebrated. Again, the prayer encourages us to look far and wide, to see what is taking place throughout the world.

For he himself ... emphasises again that the Eucharist comes to us from Christ. This is perhaps an appropriate moment to recall the emphasis that Saint Paul similarly gives to this fact:

For I received from the Lord what I also delivered to you, that the Lord Jesus on the night when he was betrayed took bread, and when he had given thanks, he broke it, and said, "This is my body which is for you. Do this in remembrance of me." In the same way also the cup, after supper, saying, "This cup is the new covenant in my blood. Do this, as often as you drink it, in remembrance of me."[127]

Literally, the Latin underlying *by whose death you willed to reconcile us to yourself* means 'by whose immolation you willed to be appeased', which seems to imply an image of God that would be difficult to defend. In fact, Vagaggini's original suggestion meant 'by whose *intercession* you willed to be appeased'. The English translation has softened the harshness of the Latin.

Translators always have to decide whether a prepositional phrase denotes something that is affirmed or something that is requested. That is, whether *Spiritu eius Sancto repleti* should be translated as asking that we *may* be filled with the Holy Spirit or saying that we *are* filled with the Holy Spirit. There is a tendency in the English translation to see such phrases, when they come into a context that follows the reception of a sacrament, as referring to something that has taken place in the sacramental encounter, rather than something that we pray may happen as a result of it. Hence, we say *we, who are ... filled with his Holy Spirit.*

The entire people

The phrase *the Order of Bishops* indicates that the bishops of the world form a single group, often called a 'college'. The Second Vatican Council laid great stress on the collegiality of bishops. In the Latin, the clergy also are spoken of as a single body – *universo clero*, which might be translated 'the whole body of the *clergy*'. In the English, however, clergy functions as a plural: that is, we would say 'all the clergy *are* invited' rather than 'all the clergy *is* invited'. With *the entire people*, we return to the singular. The result is that the bishops and the people seem to be considered corporately, but the clergy as individuals. This can lead some celebrants to add other groups, as if this were an open-ended list. In fact, the three bodies of the bishops, the clergy and the people make up the entire Church. To add to this list is to misunderstand its structure.

The entire people you have gained for your own is based on 1 Peter 2:9:

> But you are a chosen race, a royal priesthood,
> a holy nation, God's own people.

The phrase here translated 'God's own people' has a slightly complicated history. The Greek text available when the Bible was first translated into Latin meant 'a people that God has acquired'. This echoes Isaiah 43:21:

> the people whom I formed for myself.

But scholars discovered a more accurate text that meant 'a people for God to acquire'. The Church's official Latin translation was altered in order to have this meaning, but the Eucharistic Prayer contains the old Latin text. This means that at the beginning of the prayer God is said to be gathering his people 'from age to age', whereas here his work of gathering is spoken of as complete. 'The entire people you are gaining for yourself' would have removed this inconsistency. It would also fit better with the prayer that follows that God will continue his ceaseless work of gathering: *gather to yourself all your children scattered throughout the world.*

Through whom you bestow on the world all that is good is a reminder that, as we confess in the Creed, all good things come from God the Father through the Son.

Fourth Eucharistic Prayer

This prayer is a twentieth-century composition, but strongly influenced by the ancient eucharistic prayers of the Christian East. In particular, it was modelled on the Anaphora of Saint Basil, so called because of the influence that Saint Basil the Great (330-379, Bishop of Caesarea in modern Turkey) was believed to have exercised on its composition. As its heading in the Missal indicates, it presents a summary of the history of salvation. Because of this, the Preface and the rest of the prayer belong together: to use another Preface with the body of Eucharistic Prayer would disrupt the flow of the narrative. The Preface is not in fact concerned with the history of salvation, but with creation, focussing on the creation of the angels, whose song, *Holy, Holy, Holy,* the Preface introduces.

Living and true

God is said to be *living* and *true* several times in Scripture. At Lystra, where an unruly crowd thought Paul and Barnabas were gods, they replied:

> Men, why are you doing this? We also are men, of like nature with you, and bring you good news, that you should turn from these vain things to a living God who made the heaven and the earth and the sea and all that is in them.[128]

And the title 'true' is heard on the lips of Our Lord himself at the Last Supper:

> And this is eternal life, that they know thee the only true God, and Jesus Christ whom thou hast sent.[129]

Saint Paul puts the two titles together when writing to the Thessalonians:

> ...you turned to God from idols, to serve a living and true God.[130]

The source of life

The source of life is a phrase from the Psalms:

> For with thee is the fountain of life;
> in thy light do we see light.[131]

Our Lord himself develops this thought when speaking to the Samaritan woman at Jacob's well:

> Every one who drinks of this water will thirst again, but whoever drinks of the water that I shall give him will never thirst. The water that I shall give him will become in him a spring of water welling up to eternal life.[132]

Many of them reminds us that some of God's angels have rejected him.[133] With *you have fashioned all your works in wisdom and in love* compare the Psalm:

> O Lord, how manifold are thy works!
> In wisdom hast thou made them all.[134]

The whole human race

Man must be understood to refer to the whole human race. This passage is based on Genesis 1:26-27, where the creation of both males and females is narrated and dominion is granted to both sexes together:

> Then God said, 'Let us make man in our image, after our likeness; and let them have dominion over the fish of the sea, and over the birds of the air, and over the cattle, and over all the earth, and over every creeping thing that creeps upon the earth.' So God created man in his own image, in the image of God he created him; male and female he created them.

In *you offered them covenant*s, 'them' must again be understood to refer to all humanity. Most of God's covenants were offered to the people of Israel, but the covenant with Noah[135] was offered to all humankind.

You so loved the world echoes Jesus' words:

> For God so loved the world that he gave his only Son, that whoever believes in him should not perish but have eternal life.[136]

With in the *fullness of time* compare the hymn in the first chapter of the Letter to the Ephesians:

> For he (i.e. God) has made known to us in all wisdom and insight the mystery of his will, according to his purpose which he set forth in Christ as a plan for the

fullness of time, to unite all things in him, things in heaven and things on earth.[137]

With *he shared our human nature in all things* but sin compare:

For we have not a high priest who is unable to sympathise with our weaknesses, but one who in every respect has been tempted as we are, yet without sinning.[138]

The liturgical text should not be taken to imply that sin is an essential part of human nature: it is due to the Fall, from the consequences of which Jesus and his Mother are exempt.

The ministry of Jesus

The brief account of Jesus' ministry is based on the words of Isaiah that Jesus read aloud in the synagogue at Nazareth, as reported in Luke's Gospel:

The Spirit of the Lord is upon me,
because he has anointed me to preach good news to the poor. He has sent me to proclaim release to the captives and recovering of sight to the blind,
to set at liberty those who are oppressed...[139]

That we might live no longer for ourselves but for him who died and rose again for us is taken almost without alteration from Saint Paul:

And he (i.e. Jesus) died for all, that those who live might live no longer for themselves but for him who for their sake died and was raised.[140]

First fruits for those who believe means that those who have received the gift of God's Holy Spirit in Christian Initiation look forward to more abundant blessings in the future. As Saint Paul says:

... we ourselves, who have the first fruits of the Spirit, groan inwardly as we wait for adoption as sons, the redemption of our bodies.[141]

It is not clear who 'his' and 'he' refer to in the English version: *bringing to perfection his work in the world, he might sanctify creation to the full,* but comparison with the Latin shows that they refer to the Holy Spirit.

The hour had come

The anticipation of Jesus' 'hour' runs right through the Gospel of John, for instance when he says to his Mother:

My hour has not yet come."[142]

As the feast of the Passover approached, he said:

The hour has come for the Son of man to be glorified.[143]

Then, as the Last Supper begins, John's Gospel says:

> Now before the feast of the Passover, when Jesus knew that his hour had come to depart out of this world to the Father, having loved his own who were in the world, he loved them to the end.[144]

The Fourth Eucharistic Prayer stays close to the words of John's Gospel as the Consecration approaches.

The fruit of the vine may seem an elaborate way of referring to wine, but the words are those of Our Lord himself:

> Truly, I say to you, I shall not drink again of the fruit of the vine until that day when I drink it new in the kingdom of God.[145]

The realm of the dead translates Latin *inferos,* which in the Apostles' Creed is translated as 'hell'. Both these translations are also found in the English version of the Catechism.[146]

Saint Paul urges the Romans to offer their bodies as a sacrifice:

> I appeal to you therefore, brethren, by the mercies of God, to present your bodies as a living sacrifice, holy and acceptable to God, which is your spiritual worship.[147]

This prayer, borrowing Paul's words, asks rather that a single body, the Church, united by God's Holy Spirit, may be *a living sacrifice* to the praise of God.

In this prayer, the intercessions have a much wider scope than in the other three, beginning with the Pope and extending to all people of good will.

Saint Paul's letters love to speak of the inheritance that God has promised us,[148] but the words a *heavenly inheritance* are inspired by the First Letter of Peter:

> Blessed be the God and Father of our Lord Jesus Christ! By his great mercy we have been born anew to a living hope through the resurrection of Jesus Christ from the dead, and to an inheritance which is imperishable, undefiled, and unfading, kept in heaven for you.[149]

At its end, the prayer returns to the theme of its opening, God's creation, now freed from the corruptions that result from the Fall.

Communion Rite and Conclusion

Luke tells how Jesus' disciples noticed him praying, and one of them said to him:

> Lord, teach us to pray, as John taught his disciples.[150]

This is the episode alluded to as the Communion Rite begins, and the priest introduces the Lord's Prayer thus:

> *At the Saviour's command*
> *and formed by divine teaching,*
> *we dare to say:*

The Lord's Prayer

These words, with their self-conscious rhetoric, contrast strikingly with the simplicity of the prayer that follows. In fact, the Latin is somewhat more convoluted than the English: its first line can be translated literally 'Commanded by saving precepts'. Much more simple and direct would be 'Jesus taught us', an option found in earlier English translations. The mannered style of the Latin, partially reproduced in the English, has a history behind it. Some early Latin-speaking Christians, heirs as they were of a prestigious literary tradition, were embarrassed by the simple language of the Gospels. How unprepossessing were the foundation documents of the Christian Church when compared with the account of the foundation of Rome given by Vergil in his great epic, the *Aeneid!*

As a reaction, Latin Christians from the beginning aimed at a lofty style in their writings, as if to show that the new Christian culture was no less worthy of respect than that of ancient Rome. This attitude has made its mark on the liturgy, for instance in the elaborate style of the Roman Canon. The Lord's Prayer with its Roman introduction show vividly the contrast between the Scriptural style and the Roman one. Roman rhetoric does not translate easily into modern English, nor are modern English speakers readily receptive to ancient Roman culture. This poses a problem for the translators. For the introduction to the Lord's Prayer they have taken a path that lies midway between a Roman Christian and a modern English style.

Both inner anxieties and outer disturbances are denoted by *distress*. The words that follow are drawn from Saint Paul:

> For the grace of God has appeared for the salvation of all men, training us to renounce irreligion and worldly passions, and to live sober, upright, and godly lives in this world, awaiting our blessed hope, the appearing of the glory of our great God and Saviour Jesus Christ,[151]

Blessed hope, then, means not an inner attitude but an objective reality which evokes our hope. This usage is not unknown to modern English: we might, for instance, say 'peace is the hope of us all'.

The acclamation with which the people conclude this prayer is very ancient, being found as a conclusion to the Lord's Prayer in the *Didache*, a catechetical manual that may date back to the end of the first Christian century. Some Christian groups still use it in this way.

There follows one of the very few public prayers in the Mass that are addressed to Christ. It is inspired by Jesus' words at the Last Supper:

> Peace I leave with you; my peace I give to you; not as the world gives do I give to you.[152]

The prayer for *unity in accordance with your will* recalls the prayer that Jesus makes to the Father later on at the Last Supper:

> I do not pray for these only, but also for those who believe in me through their word, that they may all be one; even as thou, Father, art in me, and I in thee, that they also may be in us, so that the world may believe that thou hast sent me. The glory which thou hast given me I have given to them, that they may be one even as we are one, I in them and thou in me, that they may become perfectly one, so that the world may know that thou hast sent me and hast loved them even as thou hast loved me.[153]

The Lamb of God

The title *Lamb of God* has already been discussed in connection with the *Gloria*. In Latin, the three invocations contain three relative clauses, but the English translation does not follow this pattern. To do so would require the people to say 'you who', which was found comical by some when it was used in interim translations in the 1960s.

When the priest says *Behold the Lamb of God*, he may be understood to be inviting the people, not only to look at the Host that he holds, but also to call to mind all the implications of that title of Our Lord. We may think of him

The vision of the lamb in heaven

walking beside the Jordan as John points him out at the beginning of his ministry. We may also think of Jesus being led to the Cross like a lamb to the slaughter. And we can think of him triumphant in heaven, the Lamb at the centre of the liturgy described in the Book of Revelation, about to marry his Bride, the Church.

The priest continues with words from Revelation that evoke this last image: as the marriage of the Lamb draws near, the author hears an angel saying:

Write this: Blessed are those who are invited to the marriage supper of the Lamb.[154]

There is a sting in these words, for it is a central theme in Revelation that not all will be saved, not all will be invited to the Lamb's wedding. The book was written for Christians who were being persecuted, to reassure them that God's loving plan would eventually triumph over the evil that surrounded and threatened them. For Christians today it can be a reminder of the persecuted church, and also a challenge to self-examination. That is, it can lead us to ask the question 'Will I be invited to the supper of the Lamb?' Such self-examination is entirely appropriate before Holy Communion, and recommended by Saint Paul:

Let a man examine himself, and so eat of the bread and drink of the cup.[155]

Lord I am not worthy

The people's response *Lord, I am not worthy that you
should enter under my roof but only say the word, and my
soul shall be healed* borrows the words of the centurion
who begged Jesus to heal his servant from a distance:

> Lord, I am not worthy to have you come under my roof;
> but only say the word, and my servant will be healed.[156]

The replacement of 'Servant' in the gospel by *soul* in
the liturgy makes the text applicable to the situation of the
communicant.

The body of Christ and *The blood of Christ,* spoken by
the person administering Holy Communion, have a similar
form to *The word of the Lord* and *The mystery of faith:*
they are not complete sentences, but acclamations inviting
a response.

Saint Augustine says that our response *Amen* to The
Body of Christ is not only a profession of faith in the
eucharistic presence of the Lord, but also an affirmation
that we are the Body of Christ, that is, his Church:

> If you wish to understand the Body of Christ, listen to
> the Apostle when he says to the faithful 'Now you are
> the body of Christ and individually members of it'[157] So
> if you are the body and members of Christ, what is on
> the Lord's table is the mystery that is yourselves: you
> receive your own mystery. You reply 'Amen' to that

which you are, and by replying you assent to it. You hear 'The Body of Christ', and you reply 'Amen'. Be a true member of the body of Christ, so that your 'Amen' may be true.[158]

The prayer of the priest as he purifies the Chalice, with its parallels between *lips* and *heart* and between *time* and *eternity,* shows the characteristic balance of Roman prayer.

Conclusion

The priest ends, as he had begun, with an invocation of the Trinity, this time in the final Blessing. The simple form of blessing may be replaced when appropriate by a longer Solemn Blessing. The use of these texts was originally reserved to bishops, and fell into disuse after the Middle Ages. Their use was revived after the Second Vatican Council, and they can now be used by any priest. Their Latin originals were written to impress, with much alliteration, assonance and internal rhyme, sound being more important than sense. For this reason, they are very difficult to translate into other languages for liturgical use.

A further alternative is to use one of the Prayers over the People. Their origin is not entirely certain, but the most likely explanation seems to be that they were said by a bishop as he left the Church at the end of Mass and passed a group of penitents who were gathered near the door, since they were not allowed into the church itself during

Mass. For this reason, these prayers are particularly, though not exclusively, associated with the Season of Lent. Before the Council, the Missal contained a Prayer over the People for nearly every day in Lent. This pattern was re-established in the Third (2002) Edition.

In the Middle Ages, the bishop's blessing was a solemn moment, attended by much ceremony. There were attempts, particularly from Rome, to curb this display, which is why a bishop's blessing is preceded by verses from the Psalms that draw attention to the Lord and away from the bishop:

> *Blessed be the name of the Lord.*
> *Now and for ever.*[159]
> *Our help is in the name of the Lord.*
> *Who made heaven and earth.*[160]

The meaning of the old Latin form of the dismissal, *Ite, missa est,* is not entirely clear, but it indicates that the people are not merely dismissed, but sent out on mission. During the pontificate of Benedict XVI, other formulae were added to bring out this emphasis more clearly.

Notes

1 Matthew 28:19-20
2 Luke 22:19
2a Compare 2 Corinthians 5:15
3 2 Corinthians 13:13
4 Acts 2:42
5 Galatians 2:9
6 2 Corinthians 6:14; 8:4; 9:13
7 1 Corinthians 1:9
8 Philippians 2:1
9 1 Corinthians 10:16-17
10 1 John 1:3
11 1 John 1:6-7
12 Romans 1:7; 1 Corinthians 1:3; 2 Corinthians 1:2; Galatians 1:3; Ephesians 1:2; Philippians 1:2; 2 Thessalonians 1:2; Philemon 3
13 Colossians 1:2; 1 Thessalonians 1:1
14 1 Peter 1,2; 2 Peter 1,2
15 Revelation 1:4
16 Ruth 2:4
17 Matthew 1:5-16
18 John 20:19; 21
19 John 20:26
20 Revelation 1:10-20
21 Galatians 6:18
22 Philippians 4:23; Philemon 25
23 2 Timothy 4:22
24 Galatians 5:16-26
25 Romans 8:15-16
26 Galatians 5:19-21

27 Galatians 5:22-23
28 Compare Acts 2:28, though Saint John Chrysostom used a text different from that recognised by modern scholars
29 Saint John Chrysostom, Sermon on Pentecost, 4
30 1 Corinthians 12:3
31 1 Corinthians 11:27-29
32 Matthew 5:23-24
32a 2 Samuel 11: 2-27
33 1 Chronicles 21:8
34 Baruch 3:2
35 Luke 4:18-19
36 Isaiah 61:1
37 Psalms 147:3
38 Matthew 9:13; cf. Mark 2:17; Luke 5:31
39 Matthew 9:13
40 Mark 14:62
41 Mark 14:62; Luke 22:69
42 Ephesians 1:20
43 Colossians 3:1. Cf. Hebrews 1:3
44 Romans 8:34. Cf. Hebrews 7:25
45 Catechism of the Catholic Church 1456
46 Wisdom 11:23
47 Saint John Chrysostom, Homily 4 on Philippians
48 Luke 2:14.

49 Liturgiam authenticam 23
50 Liturgiam authenticam 56
51 John 1:29. Cf. John 1:36.
52 Isaiah 53: 4-7.
53 Jeremiah 11:19
54 De Oratione 8
55 Aeterna lux, divinitas, translated by Edward Caswall
56 Genesis 15:1
57 Isaiah 66:5
58 Ezechiel 37:15
59 1 Peter 1:25
60 Luke 1:38
61 John 1:1
62 Sacrosanctum Concilium 7
63 Summa Theologiae, IIa IIae, I, 9
64 Catechism 185
65 2 Corinthians 3:17
66 2 Corinthians 3:6
67 John 15:26
68 2 Peter 1:21
69 December 29, Prayer over the Offerings
70 John 6:35; 48
71 Romans 1:25
72 Romans 9:5
73 1 Corinthians 10:3-4
74 John 6:55
75 Daniel 3:26
76 Daniel 3:27
77 Daniel 3:39-40

78 Presbyterorum Ordinis 2
79 2 Corinthians 5:15
80 Daniel 3:21
81 Presbyterorum Ordinis 2
82 Catechism 331
82a Hebrews 13:12-15
83 Isaiah 6:1-5
84 Revelation 4:8
85 Revelation 12:7
86 Matthew 21:9;15; Mark 11:9-10; John 12:13
87 Matthew 21:9; Mark 11:9; John 12:13; cf. Luke 19:38
88 Acts 4:11
89 Psalms 118:24
89 He 13:12-15
90 Romans 12:1
91 1 Corinthians 10:17 as translated by Nicholas King, who brings out the point clearly.
92 Luke 9:16
92a Luke 9:16
93 Isaiah 25:6
94 Matthew 26:28
95 Mark 14:24
96 Isaiah 53:12
97 1 Timothy 3:16
98 1 Corinthians 11:26
99 1 Peter 2:9
100 John 6:35; 48
101 Psalm 116:12-13
102 Genesis 4:1-16
103 Hebrews 11:4
104 Genesis 22:1-14
105 Hebrews 11:17
106 Genesis 14:18-19
107 Psalms 110:4b
108 Revelation 8:3
109 Revelation 9:13
110 Revelation 11:1
111 Revelation 16:7
112 1 Corinthians 10:18
113 Sacrosanctum Concilium 81.
114 Ephesians 3:21
115 Commentary on Luke 7:95
116 Sermon 60
116a Liber divinorum operum 3, 4, 5
116b 1 John 4:12
117 Romans 6:5
118 Romans 6:3-4
119 Psalms 4:6
120 Psalms 89:15
121 Psalms 90:8
123 Philippians 2:9
124 Psalms 19:1.
125 Daniel 3:57-58.
126 Malachi 1:10b-11
127 1 Corinthians 11:23-25
128 Acts 14:14
129 John 17:3
130 1 Thessalonians 1:9
131 Psalms 36:9
132 John 4:13-14
133 Catechism 391-395
134 Psalms 104:24
135 Genesis 9:9-17
136 John 3:16
137 Ephesians 1:9-10
138 Hebrews 4:15.
139 Luke 4:18
140 2 Corinthians 5:15
141 Romans 8:23
142 John 2:4
143 John 12:23
144 John 13:1
145 Mark 14:25. Cf. Matthew 26:29 and Luke 22:18
146 Catechism 632-637.
147 Romans 12:1
148 e.g. Galatians 3:18; Ephesians 1:14; 18; Colossians 1:12; 3:24; Cf. Hebrews 9:15
149 1 Peter 1:3-4
150 Luke 11:1
151 Titus 2:11-13.
152 John 14:27
153 John 17:20-23.
154 Revelation 19:9
155 1 Corinthians 11:28
156 Matthew 8:8; Luke 7:6-7
157 1 Corinthians 12:27
158 Augustine, Sermon 272
159 Psalms 113:2
160 Psalms 124:8